HERTFORDSHIRE LIBRARY SERVICE
BOOKS
WITHDRAWN FOR SALE
PRICE

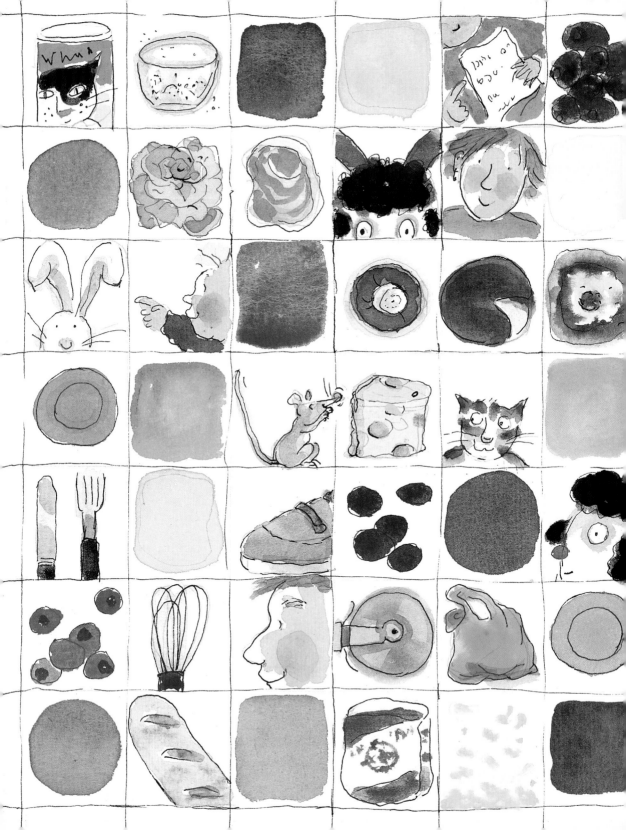

To Parents and Teachers:

We hope you and the children will enjoy reading this story in English and Spanish. It is simply told, but not *simplified,* so that both versions are quite natural. However, there is a lot of repetition for practising pronunciation, for helping develop memory skills, and for reinforcing comprehension.

At the back of the book, there is a simple picture dictionary with key words as well as a basic pronunciation guide to the whole story.

Here are a few suggestions for using the book:

• First, read the story aloud in English to become familiar with it. Treat it like any other picture book. Look at the drawings, talk about the story, the characters, and so on.

• Then look at the picture dictionary and repeat the key words in Spanish. Make this an active exercise. Ask the children to say the words out loud instead of reading them.

• Go back and read the story again, this time in English and Spanish. Don't worry if your pronunciation isn't quite correct. Just have fun trying it out. If necessary, check the guide at the back of the book, but you'll soon pick up how to say the Spanish words.

• When you think you and the children are ready, try reading the story in Spanish. Ask the children to say it with you. Only ask them to read it if they seem eager to try. The spelling could be confusing and discourage them.

• Above all, encourage the children and give them lots of praise. They are usually quite unselfconscious, so let them be children and playact, try out different voices, and have fun. This is an excellent way to build confidence for acquiring foreign language skills.

Published by b small publishing
Pinewood, 3a Coombe Ridings, Kingston-upon-Thames, Surrey KT2 7JT
www.bsmall.co.uk
© b small publishing, 1998
1 2 3 4 5
All rights reserved.
Design: *Lone Morton*   Editorial: *Catherine Bruzzone*   Production: *Madeleine Ehm*
Printed in China by WKT Co. Ltd.
ISBN 1 902915 28 3 (paperback)
British Library Cataloguing in Publication Data. A catalogue record for this book is available from the British Library.

What's for supper?

¿Qué hay para cenar?

Mary Risk
Pictures by Carol Thompson
Spanish by Rosa Martín

We're making supper tonight,
Mum.

Esta noche vamos a preparar la
cena *nosotros*, mamá.

It's going to be a surprise.

Va a ser una sorpresa.

Do we need cheese?

¿Necesitamos queso?

Yes, we need cheese, and ham too.

Sí, necesitamos queso y también jamón.

Do we need flour?

¿Necesitamos harina?

Yes.

Sí.

And potatoes?
Do we need them?

¿Y patatas?
¿Necesitamos patatas?

No, we don't need potatoes.

No, no necesitamos patatas.

But we need tomatoes
and mushrooms.

Pero necesitamos tomates y
champiñones.

Let's put some olives in it, too!

¡Vamos a ponerle unas aceitunas, también!

Oh no! I don't like olives.

¡Ay no! No me gustan las aceitunas.

How much is all that?

¿Cuánto es todo?

What are you going to make?
Please tell me. Please!

No! It's a surprise!

¿Qué vas a hacer?
¡Vamos, dímelo! ¡Por favor!

¡No! ¡Es una sorpresa!

Here we are home again.

Ya estamos de vuelta en casa.

Don't come into the kitchen, Mum.

No entres en la cocina, mamá.

Supper's ready. It's…

La cena está lista. Es…

a pizza!

¡una pizza!

Pronouncing Spanish

Don't worry if your pronunciation isn't quite correct. The important thing is to be willing to try. The pronunciation guide here is based on the Spanish accent used in Spain. Although it cannot be completely accurate, it certainly will be a great help.

• Read the guide as naturally as possible, as if it were English.

• Put stress on the letters in *italics,* e.g., ko*thee*na.

If you can, ask a Spanish-speaking person to help and move on as soon as possible to speaking the words without the guide.

Note: Spanish adjectives usually have two forms, one for masculine and one for feminine nouns. They often look very similar but are pronounced slightly differently, e.g., **listo** and **lista** (see next page).

Words Las palabras
lass pal-*ab*rass

to cook supper
preparar la cena
praypah-*rahr* lah *thay*na

tonight
esta noche
essta nocheh

surprise
la sorpresa
lah sorpraysa

cheese
el queso
el keh-so

ham
el jamón
el hamon

flour
la harina
lah areena

tomato
el tomate
el tomah-teh

potato
la patata
lah patah-ta

olive
la aceituna
lah athay-toonah

mushroom
el champiñón
el champeen-yon

pizza
la pizza
lah peet-sah

ready
listo/lista
leesto/ leesta

home/house
la casa
lah *kah*-sa

Mum
mamá
mam*ma*

Dad
papá
pa*pah*

kitchen
la cocina
lah ko*thee*na

yes
sí
see

no
no
noh

please
por favor
poor fa*vor*

A simple guide to pronouncing this Spanish story

¿Qué hay para cenar?
keh aye *par*-ah thay-*nar*

Esta noche vamos a preparar
*es*ta *noch*eh *va*moss ah praypah-*rahr*

la cena *nosotros*, mamá.
lah *thay*na no*sso*tross, mam*ma*

Va a ser una sorpresa.
vah ah sair *oo*na sor*pray*sa

¿Necesitamos queso?
nethessee-*ta*moss *keh*-so

**Sí, necesitamos queso y
también jamón.**
see, nethessee-*ta*moss *keh*-so, ee
tamb-*yen* ham*on*

¿Necesitamos harina?
nethessee-*ta*moss a*ree*na

Sí.
see

¿Y patatas?
ee pa*tah*-tass

¿Necesitamos patatas?
nethessee-*ta*moss pa*tah*-tass

No, no necesitamos patatas.
noh, noh nethessee-*ta*moss
pa*tah*-tass

Pero necesitamos tomates
pair-ro nethessee-*ta*moss to*mah*-tess

y champiñones.
ee champeen-*yon*ess

**¡Vamos a ponerle unas aceitunas
también!**
*va*moss ah pon-*air*leh *oo*nass
athay-*too*nass tamb-*yen*

**¡Ay no! No me gustan las
aceitunas.**
aye noh, noh meh *goo*stan lass
athay-*too*nass

¿Cuánto es todo?
*kwan*to ess *toh*-do

¿Qué vas a hacer?
keh vas ah ah-*thair*

¡Vamos, dímelo! ¡Por favor!
*va*moss, *dee*-mehlo, poor fav*or*

¡No! ¡Es una sorpresa!
noh, ess *oo*na sor*pray*sa

Ya estamos de vuelta en casa.
ya est*a*moss deh *voo*-el ta en
kah-sa

No entres en la cocina, mamá.
noh *en*tress en lah ko*thee*na, mam*ma*

La cena está lista. Es...
lah *thay*na ess-*tah lee*sta, ess

¡una pizza!
*oo*na *peet*-sah

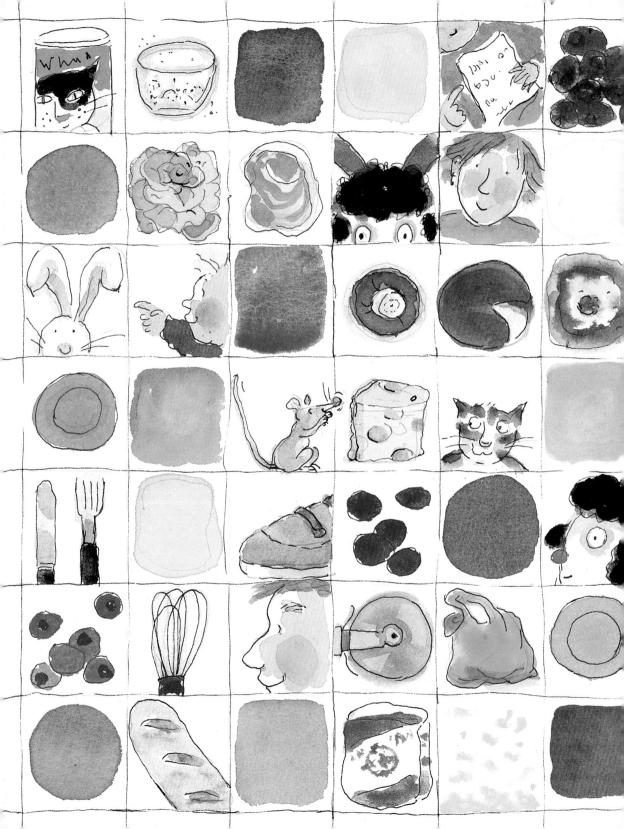